How To Use This Study Guide

This five-lesson study guide corresponds to *"The Ministry of Angels — How To Activate Angels To Help You Right Now" With Rick Renner* (Renner TV). Each lesson in this study guide covers a topic that is addressed during the program series, with questions and references supplied to draw you deeper into your own private study of the Scriptures on this subject.

To derive the most benefit from this study guide, consider the following:

First, watch or listen to the program prior to working through the corresponding lesson in this guide. (Programs can also be viewed at **renner.org** by clicking on the Media/Archives links or on our Renner Ministries YouTube channel.)

Second, take the time to look up the scriptures included in each lesson. Prayerfully consider their application to your own life.

Third, use a journal or notebook to make note of your answers to each lesson's Study Questions and Practical Application challenges.

Fourth, invest specific time in prayer and in the Word of God to consult with the Holy Spirit. Write down the scriptures or insights He reveals to you.

Finally, take action! Whatever the Lord tells you to do according to His Word, do it.

For added insights on this subject, it is recommended that you obtain Joseph Z's book *Servants of Fire,* Terry Law's book *The Truth About Angels,* and Rick Renner's book *Last-Days Survival Guide: A Scriptural Handbook To Prepare You for These Perilous Times.* You may also select from Rick's other available resources by placing your order at **renner.org** or by calling 1-800-742-5593.

TOPIC

Angels Meet Physical Needs and Provide Strength

SCRIPTURES

1. **Hebrews 1:14** — Are they [angels] not all ministering spirits, sent forth to minister for them who shall be heirs of salvation?

2. **Hebrews 12:22** — …innumerable….

3. **Matthew 4:11** — Then the devil leaveth him, and, behold, angels came and ministered unto him.

4. **Mark 1:13** — And he was there in the wilderness forty days, tempted of Satan; and was with the wild beasts; and the angels ministered unto him.

5. **Luke 22:43** — And there appeared an angel unto him from heaven, strengthening him.

6. **Psalm 103:20** — Bless the Lord, ye his angels, that excel in strength, that do his commandments, hearkening unto the voice of his word.

GREEK WORDS

1. "ministering" — λειτουργικός (*leitourgikos*): sacred ministry, depicting service to God and to others; one who is authorized to do sacred service, such as Old Testament priests who were to assist with the various needs of those in the temple; hence, God has assigned to angels the sacred task of serving the various needs of those who are heirs of salvation

2. "sent forth" — ἀποστέλλω (*apostello*): dispatched on assignment to represent a high-ranking power; one empowered to carry out the specific duties that are assigned to him

3. "minister" — διακονία (*diakonia*): a high-level servant; a sophisticated and highly trained servant who served the needs of others; a servant whose primary responsibility was to serve food and wait on tables; pictures a waiter or waitress who painstakingly attends to the needs, wishes, and desires of his or her client; servants who professionally pleased clients; a type of serving that was honorable, pleasurable, and

A Note From Rick Renner

I am on a personal quest to see a "revival of the Bible" so people can establish their lives on a firm foundation that will stand strong and endure the test as end-time storm winds begin to intensify.

In order to experience a revival of the Bible in your personal life, it is important to take time each day to read, receive, and apply its truths to your life. James tells us that if we will continue in the perfect law of liberty — refusing to be forgetful hearers, but determined to be doers — we will be blessed in our ways. As you watch or listen to the programs in this series and work through this corresponding study guide, I trust you will search the Scriptures and allow the Holy Spirit to help you hear something new from God's Word that applies specifically to your life. I encourage you to be a doer of the Word He reveals to you. Whatever the cost, I assure you — it will be worth it.

> Thy words were found, and I did eat them;
> and thy word was unto me the joy and rejoicing of mine heart:
> for I am called by thy name, O Lord God of hosts.
> — Jeremiah 15:16

Your brother and friend in Jesus Christ,

Rick Renner

The Ministry of Angels
How To Activate Angels To Help You Right Now

Copyright © 2023 by Rick Renner
1814 W. Tacoma St.
Broken Arrow, OK 74012-1406

Published by Rick Renner Ministries
www.renner.org

ISBN 13: 978-1-6675-0598-5

eBook ISBN 13: 978-1-6675-0599-2

done in a fashion that made the people being served feel as if they were nobility

4. "ministered"— διάκονος (*diakonos*): a high-level servant; sophisticated and highly trained servants who served the needs of others; a servant whose primary responsibility was to serve food and wait on tables; pictures a waiter or waitress who painstakingly attends to the needs, wishes, and desires of his or her client; servants who professionally pleased clients; a type of serving that was honorable, pleasurable, and done in a fashion that made the people being served feel as if they were nobility

5. "strengthen"— ἐνισχύω (*enischuo*): a compound of the words ἐν (*en*) and ἰσχύω (*ischuo*); the preposition ἐν (*en*) means in, and the word ἰσχύω (*ischuo*) means might or strength; the word ἰσχύω (*ischuo*) denotes men with great muscular abilities, such as champions or heroes; but when these two words ἐν (*en*) and ἰσχύω (*ischuo*) are compounded, the new word means to impart strength, to empower someone, to fill a person with physical vigor, or to give someone a renewed vitality; a person may have been feeling exhausted and depleted, but suddenly he receives a robust blast of energy that instantly recharges him

SYNOPSIS

The five lessons in this study titled *The Ministry of Angels — How To Activate Angels To Help You Right Now* will focus on the following topics:

• Angels Meet Physical Needs and Provide Strength

• Angels Give Supernatural Guidance

• Angels Provide Protection and Deliverance

• Angels Make Divine Announcements and Release God's Divine Judgment

• Angels Perform Superhuman Feats and Worship God

Did you know angels are available to help you *right now*? There are many strange and unscriptural teachings available on the subject of angels, but what does the *Bible* say? In this five-part series, you will learn what the Bible teaches about angels and how to activate angelic assistance.

The emphasis of this lesson:

Many people are aware of the existence of angels but *unaware* of the intended role of angels in the life of the believer. Angels have been tasked by God to do many things (even Jesus needed angelic assistance!), but it is vital that we understand what angels do and what angels *never* do.

Sacred Ministry

According to the New Testament, angels are entrusted with the care of the *elect* and the *heirs of salvation*. We read about this in Hebrews 1:14, which says:

> Are they [angels] not all ministering spirits, sent forth to minister for them who shall be heirs of salvation?

If you are saved, you are an heir of salvation. So this verse describes *YOU!*

This verse provides important information about the charge that has been entrusted to angels. First, verse 14 says, "Are they [angels] not all *ministering* spirits…?" You may ask, *What kind of ministry are they authorized to do?* The word "ministering" describes *sacred ministry*. Angels are authorized to do sacred service. The word translated "ministering" is also used in the Old Testament to describe *the priests charged with assisting worshipers with various needs.* Here we find that God has assigned to angels the sacred task of serving the various needs of those who are the heirs of salvation — that's *YOU!*

Next, this verse explains the angels have been "sent forth." This phrase is translated from the Greek word *apostello*, which describes *one that is dispatched on an assignment to represent a high-ranking power*. It also depicts *one empowered to carry out a specific duty assigned to him*. This means angels have been dispatched by God; they are His representatives; and they have been assigned specific duties.

Hebrews 1:14 goes on to say that angels "minister for them who shall be heirs of salvation." The word "minister" is translated from the Greek word *diakonia*, which describes *a high-level servant* or *a sophisticated and highly trained servant who serves the needs of others*. The word *diakonia* was first used in reference to a servant whose primary responsibility was to serve food and wait on tables. It pictures *a waiter or waitress who painstakingly attends to the needs, wishes, and desires of his or her client*. It denotes *a servant whose profession it was to please clients* or *a type of serving that was honorable, pleasurable, and done in a fashion that made the people being served feel as if they were nobility.* This tells us that angels are high-level, highly trained servants who have been sent forth to meet the needs of believers. Not only have angels been dispatched to meet your needs and assist with the various things you are facing in life, but they have been sent forth to *professionally* meet those needs and serve you.

You may have asked, *Do angels ever help wicked people?* The answer is no. There is not a single verse in the Bible that describes angels helping those who are wicked. But indeed, there are many verses that say angels are *against* the wicked. Angels are servants at the table of God's elect who are the heirs of salvation.

How Many Angels Are There?

God sends His angels to meet His people's needs, but He also sends angels to strengthen the weary, give supernatural guidance (which frequently occurs through dreams or visions), provide protection and deliverance from harm, carry out superhuman feats, make special announcements, release divine judgment, and worship. Because there are so many believers around the world, many people wonder how the angels are able to carry out such a myriad of assignments for such a large number of people. The Bible never explicitly says how many angels there are. However, Hebrews 12:22 says that the heavenly hosts of angels are "innumerable." There are so many angels that they cannot be counted! We can be assured that these innumerable angels stand ready to assist you and are available.

A Warning Against Preoccupation With Angels

The Colossian church had experienced so-called "angels" appearing and teaching false doctrine, so in his letter to the Colossians, the apostle Paul warned against having a preoccupation with angels (*see* Colossians 2:18). A similar occurrence also happened in the region of Galatia (*see* Galatians 1:8).

During the First Century, Paul and the other apostles were often confronting teachings that had purportedly come from angels. What the apostles understood was that angels never teach, and they never preach the Word of God. We find in the Scriptures that angels will make divine announcements, but those announcements are always verbatim — word for word — as given to them directly from the mouth of God. Angels are never — *not ever* — charged with the business of teaching and preaching the Gospel. It is important that you understand this truth. For instance, if you hear of someone who has received a revelation that was taught to him or her by an angel, you can be sure it will lead to false doctrine. Be on your guard concerning such teachings.

Another common misconception is the depiction of female angels. There is not a single example — in the Old or New Testament — of a female angel. They are always described as being *male* in character and appearance. We *must* stick with the Bible on this subject, and we must not allow ourselves to become preoccupied with angels or false teachings and doctrines regarding them. Paul and the other apostles were very adamant about this.

In this series, we will discuss what angels do today. But it is interesting to note that in the *future*, angels will have additional responsibilities. For example, angels will be sent forth to separate the "sheep" from the "goats" (*see* Matthew 13:41,42,50). Also, angels will accompany Jesus at His Second Coming (*see* 2 Thessalonians 1:7,8). But for this teaching, we will focus on what angels do for the saints *today*.

Angels Minister to Physical Needs

The first angelic assignment we will examine is that of meeting *physical needs*. In Matthew 4:11 and Mark 1:13, we read that when Jesus concluded his 40-day fast in the wilderness, a number of angels appeared to Him to meet His physical needs.

> **Then the devil leaveth him and, *behold*, angels came and ministered unto him.**
> **— Matthew 4:11**

The word "behold" means *Wow!* Matthew was so amazed by what happened, that as he was recording this event, he said, "*Wow!* Listen to this — behold — angels came and ministered unto Him!" Mark recorded the same event this way: "And he was there in the wilderness forty days, tempted of Satan; and was with the wild beasts; and the angels ministered unto him" (Mark 1:13).

Both Matthew and Mark said angels came to minister to Jesus, and in both events, the word "ministered" is translated from the word *diakonos*, which is the same word we saw earlier in this lesson. Again, it describes *a high-level servant that is sophisticated and highly trained* or *a servant that has been sent forth to serve the needs of others.* It pictures *a waiter or waitress who painstakingly attends to the needs, wishes, and desires of his or her clients* or *a servant whose profession is to please clients.* The word *diakonos* also depicts a type of serving that was honorable, pleasurable, and done in a fashion that made the people being served feel as if they were nobility.

After 40 days of fasting in the wilderness, Jesus was so physically tired that the angels came and ministered to Him. They became like waiters at the table asking how they could be of service to Jesus; they came to meet His physical needs. This emphatically means that those angels took on the role of servants and ministered to Jesus' *tangible* needs.

Angels Provide Strength

In Luke 22:43, we read that angels provide strength. Jesus was alone and under great pressure in the Garden of Gethsemane. The Word says,

And there appeared an angel unto him from heaven, strengthening him.
— **Luke 22:43**

God provided supernatural assistance in the form of an angel who came to strengthen Jesus in His moment of need. Likewise, angels are available to strengthen *you.* The word translated "strengthen" in Luke 22:43 is from the Greek word *enischuo*, which is a compound of the words *en*, which means *in*, and *ischuo*, which means *might* or *strength.* The word *ischuo* depicts *men of great muscular abilities like champions or heroes*, but when these two words are compounded, the new word — *enischuo* — means *to impart strength, to empower, to fill a person with physical vigor*, or *to give someone renewed vitality.* It depicts a person who may have been feeling exhausted or depleted, but suddenly he receives a robust blast of energy that instantly charges him so he can continue.

This means that when Jesus' disciples were not faithful to Him — when it seemed that they had abandoned Him and couldn't be depended upon in His hour of need — God provided an angel who *empowered, recharged,* and *renewed* Jesus' vitality so He could victoriously face the most difficult hour of His life.

If *you* are feeling exhausted or depleted, know that you have an inexhaustible source of strength in the Holy Spirit living inside you. But God will also send angels to give you robust strength and vitality to recharge and revive you.

So we know that angels can be sent to strengthen those who are weary. But how do you *activate* the various ministries of angels?

How To Activate the Ministry of Angels

In Psalm 103:20, the Bible says, "Bless the Lord, ye his angels, that excel in strength, that do his commandments, hearkening unto the voice of his word." According to this verse, you activate angels any time you declare the Word of God. Take Psalm 91, for example — it says He will give His angels charge over you to keep you in all your ways, lest you dash your foot against a stone (*see* Psalm 91:11,12). That passage declares that angels are available to keep you in every way, and when you quote that verse, angels suddenly stand at attention, ready to take orders because they hear the Word of God.

An Angelic Encounter

In the program, Rick shared the following example of an angelic encounter from his life:

> Many years ago, the ministry was facing a very difficult time financially, and even though worrying is a sin, is a waste of emotion, and isn't productive, I had been worrying. And as a result, I was depleted physically. The giving of our partners had dipped for some reason, so I didn't have the money to pay the TV station directors for our broadcasts.

> I was brokenhearted because I was going to have to look into the faces of those TV station directors and tell them I didn't have enough money to pay for the next month of programs. On top of that, I was thinking of all the viewers who were hearing the Word of God for the first time in their lives on our program. The thought that it might be discontinued broke my heart.

> I remember it was the middle of winter, and the meeting was scheduled very late at night at a hotel in downtown Moscow. I couldn't bring myself to look into the eyes of those TV directors

and tell them I didn't have the money, so I asked to be excused. I walked out on Tverskaya Street (the main street that runs into the Kremlin), stopped at a construction site, leaned against a cold, metal railing, and began to cry. I said, "Lord, You've got to do something for me. I need your strength; I'm depleted. I don't know what to do, and I don't have the strength to go on."

I remembered the example of the angel appearing to strengthen Jesus in His hour of need. I said, "Lord, please do for me what the angel did for Jesus." And in that moment, the angels were activated, Heaven opened, and strength was downloaded into me. My gusto was renewed!

Suddenly, I was just like Clark Kent coming out of the phone booth as Superman. Something miraculous happened to me, and instantaneously I was charged and renewed with strength. According to Hebrews 1:14, God provided angelic ministry for me because I am an heir of salvation. On that night, the angels ministered to me just like they ministered to Jesus in the wilderness and in the Garden of Gethsemane.

In fact, I was so recharged with strength and power that I wiped the tears from my eyes, walked back up the street to that hotel, went upstairs to where the directors were meeting, and said, "You know what, I don't have the cash with me today, but I'll get it to you in just a few days." My faith and my strength were renewed!

Supernatural strengthening is one of the aspects of angelic ministry and it is available to *YOU*! If you're feeling depleted, you can recall the example of what the angels did for Jesus in the wilderness and in the Garden of Gethsemane, and you can say, "Lord, do for me what You did for Jesus." Angels excel in providing strength, and they will fulfill the Scripture in your life just as they did for Jesus. If you are feeling weary, they will meet your physical and tangible needs and provide strength to you. The *moment* you speak the Word of God, they will hearken to the commandment of His Word, and they will go to work for you!

STUDY QUESTIONS

Study to shew thyself approved unto God, a workman that
needeth not to be ashamed, rightly dividing the word of truth.
— 2 Timothy 2:15

1. According to Hebrews 1:14, what is the primary assignment given to angels? List at least three additional tasks regularly assigned to angels.

2. In Galatians 1:8 and Colossians 2:18, we see that Paul and the other apostles were confronting a particular problem in the churches. What was that problem, and why is it important that we heed the same warnings given to those churches?

PRACTICAL APPLICATION

But be ye doers of the word, and not hearers only,
deceiving your own selves.
— James 1:22

1. What are your physical needs? Have you been trying to meet them in your own strength? We've learned in this lesson that you don't have to do it all alone and that there are angels available *right now* to meet your physical needs. They simply need to be activated. Take some time to write down your three most urgent physical needs, and then search the Scriptures for what God has said regarding each one. Declare those verses out loud over your needs whenever they come to mind this week.

2. Have you ever felt exhausted or depleted? What steps did you take to revive your strength? After reading this lesson, how has your perspective changed, and how can you better address physical exhaustion and depletion in the future? Review the accounts of Jesus' physically weakest moments and note how God responded with angelic assistance.
   - Matthew 4:1-11
   - Mark 1:12,13
   - Luke 22:39-43

3. Are you aware of a time when you or someone you know was *supernaturally* recharged? Describe your experience. Is it possible — or even *likely* — it was the result of angelic ministry?

TOPIC

Angels Give Supernatural Guidance

SCRIPTURES

1. **Hebrews 1:14** — Are they [angels] not all ministering spirits, sent forth to minister for them who shall be heirs of salvation?

2. **Hebrews 12:22** — ...innumerable....

3. **Matthew 2:13** — And when they were departed, behold, the angel of the Lord appeareth to Joseph in a dream, saying, Arise, and take the young child and his mother, and flee into Egypt, and be thou there until I bring thee word: for Herod will seek the young child to destroy him.

4. **Matthew 2:19,20** — But when Herod was dead, behold, an angel of the Lord appeareth in a dream to Joseph in Egypt, saying, Arise, and take the young child and his mother, and go into the land of Israel: for they are dead which sought the young child's life.

5. **Acts 8:26** — And the angel of the Lord spake unto Philip, saying, Arise, and go toward the south unto the way that goeth down from Jerusalem unto Gaza, which is desert.

6. **Acts 8:27-31, 37-40** — And he arose and went: and, behold, a man of Ethiopia, an eunuch of great authority under Candace queen of the Ethiopians, who had the charge of all her treasure, and had come to Jerusalem for to worship, was returning, and sitting in his chariot read Esaias the prophet. Then the Spirit said unto Philip, Go near, and join thyself to this chariot. And Philip ran thither to him, and heard him read the prophet Esaias, and said, Understandest thou what thou readest? And he said, How can I, except some man should guide me? And he desired Philip that he would come up and sit with him.... And Philip said, If thou believest with all thine heart, thou mayest. And he answered and said, I believe that Jesus Christ is the Son of God. And he commanded the chariot to stand still: and they went down both into the water, both Philip and the eunuch; and he baptized him. And when they were come up out of the water, the Spirit of the Lord caught away Philip, that the eunuch saw him no

more: and he went on his way rejoicing. But Philip was found at Azotus: and passing through he preached in all the cities, till he came to Caesarea.

7. **Psalm 103:20** — Bless the Lord, ye his angels, that excel in strength, that do his commandments, hearkening unto the voice of his word.

GREEK WORDS

1. "ministering" — λειτουργικός (*leitourgikos*): sacred ministry, depicting service to God and to others; one who is authorized to do sacred service, such as Old Testament priests who were to assist with the various needs of those in the temple; hence, God has assigned to angels the sacred task of serving the various needs of those who are heirs of salvation

2. "sent forth" — ἀποστέλλω (*apostello*): dispatched on assignment to represent a high-ranking power; one empowered to carry out the specific duties that are assigned to him

3. "minister" — διακονία (*diakonia*): a high-level servant; sophisticated and highly trained servant who served the needs of others; a servant whose primary responsibility was to serve food and wait on tables; pictures a waiter or waitress who painstakingly attends to the needs, wishes, and desires of his or her client; servants who professionally pleased clients; a type of serving that was honorable, pleasurable, and done in a fashion that made the people being served feel as if they were nobility

SYNOPSIS

There are examples of angels providing supernatural guidance in both the Old and New Testaments. An angel appeared to Joseph in a dream, and an angel appeared in physical form to Philip, telling him to turn south from Jerusalem. Whether in dreams and visions or physically in person, angels can provide divine instruction and guidance for God's people.

The emphasis of this lesson:

Once Philip the evangelist obeyed the angel's first direction, he was positioned to receive the next one. Sometimes you must be in the right place before you receive the next instruction from the Lord.

Who Angels Minister To

In the previous lesson, we learned that angels are available to meet physical and tangible needs, and they are also available to provide strength to the weary. Angels are entrusted with the care of the *elect* and the *heirs of salvation* — that means *YOU!* We read about this in the anchor verse, Hebrews 1:14, which says:

Are they [angels] **not all ministering spirits, sent forth to minister for them who shall be heirs of salvation?**

The word "ministering" denotes *sacred ministry*. It was also used in the Old Testament Greek Septuagint to describe *the priests charged with assisting worshipers in the temple with various needs.* God has assigned to angels the sacred task of serving the various needs of those who are the heirs of salvation. If you are a believer, *you* are an heir of salvation and God has assigned angels to serve *your* needs.

Next, we see that the angels have been "sent forth." This phrase is translated from the Greek word *apostello*, which describes *one who is dispatched on an assignment to represent a high-ranking power.* It also depicts *one empowered to carry out a specific duty assigned to him.* This means angels have been dispatched by God, they are His representatives, and they have been assigned specific duties — concerning *you.*

Hebrews 1:14 goes on to say angels "minister for them who shall be heirs of salvation." The word "minister" is translated from the Greek word *diakonia*, which describes *a high-level servant* or *a sophisticated and highly trained servant who serves the needs of others.* It pictures *a waiter or waitress who painstakingly attends to the needs, wishes, and desires of his or her client, a servant whose profession it was to please clients;* or *a type of serving that was honorable, pleasurable, and done in a fashion that made the people being served feel as if they were nobility.* This means angels are not just here without an assignment, but they are highly trained, they've been sent forth to professionally serve you, and they have been commissioned to meet your needs and desires — and to treat you like nobility!

It is interesting to note that there is not a single example in the Old or New Testament of an angel helping a wicked person. However, there are many instances of angels doing a lot to *stop* the wicked. Remember, angels are sent to help those who are heirs of salvation.

The primary assignments of angels are to meet God's people's needs, strengthen the weary, give supernatural guidance, provide protection and deliverance from harm, carry out superhuman feats, make special announcements, release divine judgment, and worship. In the previous lesson, we covered two primary assignments of angels: to meet physical needs and to provide strength.

Angels Provide Strength and Minister to Physical Needs

In Matthew 4:11 and Mark 1:13, we read that when Jesus concluded His 40-day fast in the wilderness, a number of angels appeared to Him to meet His physical needs.

> **Then the devil leaveth him and, behold, angels came and ministered unto him.**
> — **Matthew 4:11**

The word "behold" means *Wow!* Matthew was so amazed by what happened, that as he was recording this event, he wrote, "Wow! Listen to this — behold — angels came and ministered unto Him!" Mark recorded the same event this way: "And he was there in the wilderness forty days, tempted of Satan; and was with the wild beasts; and the angels ministered unto him" (Mark 1:13).

In Luke 22:43, we see a clear example of an angel providing strength for someone. Here Jesus was alone and under great pressure in the Garden of Gethsemane: "And there appeared an angel unto him from heaven, strengthening him."

God provided supernatural assistance in the form of an angel who came to strengthen Jesus in His moment of need. The word translated "strengthen" in Luke 22:43 is from the Greek word *enischuo* which is a compound of the words *en*, which means *in*, and *ischuo*, which means *might* or *strength*. The word *ischuo* depicts *men of great muscular abilities* like champions or heroes, but when these two words are compounded, the new word — *enischuo* — means *to impart strength, to empower, to fill a person with physical vigor*, and *to give someone renewed vitality*. It depicts a person who may have been feeling exhausted or depleted, but suddenly he receives a robust blast of energy that instantly charges him so he can continue on. Likewise, angels are available to strengthen *you*.

In Psalm 103:20, the Bible says, "Bless the Lord, ye his angels, that excel in strength, that do his commandments, hearkening unto the voice of his word." According to this verse, you activate angels any time you declare the Word of God. Take Psalm 91 for example — it says He will give His angels charge over you to keep you in all your ways, lest you dash your foot against a stone (*see* Psalm 91:11,12). When you quote that verse, angels suddenly stand at attention because they hear the Word of God. They are activated to perform this ministry for you.

The Bible does not explicitly say how many angels there are, but we know from Hebrews 12:22 that there is an innumerable company of angels. So it should not surprise you if you have an encounter with an angel from time to time!

An Angelic Encounter

In the program, Rick shared another example of an angelic encounter he has experienced:

> Many years ago, Denise and I were ministering in the United States, and I was very physically tired. I was so depleted of strength that when I got up on that Saturday morning, knowing I needed to get on a plane and fly to a city where I was to minister the next day in a church service, I said, "Lord, I am so tired and physically depleted. Would You please do something so that I can just stay home today?" But I was scheduled to go, so I went to the airport. When I got there, the person at the counter said, "You know, it's very strange, but an unusual weather system just blew in and no planes can go in that direction."
>
> So I called the pastor and informed him that I was unable to come because my flight was being canceled. He told me to try going through Dallas, so I went back to the airport counter and asked about it. The person at the counter said, "You know, it's very unusual; now a weather system is coming to Dallas, and you can't fly in that direction either.
>
> When I informed the pastor, he said to try going through Denver, so I asked the attendant about that. But the person said, "This is very bizarre. Now there is a strange weather system that has come in through Denver. Sir, you're locked in; you can't go anywhere. You can't go east; you can't go west; you can't go south; you can't

go north. Sir, you are just going to have to stay home." Considering how physically tired and depleted I was, and the prayer I'd prayed just hours before, I was *so excited*.

That afternoon I decided to take Denise to lunch at a cafeteria-style restaurant, and while Denise waited at the table, I paid for the food at the counter. Suddenly, I heard a person say, "I know all about you." We had never met, but this person began to tell me details about my life that no one knew but me.

Then the stranger said, "You know *you* are the reason for this weather system that suddenly came into town. It's because of you. It's because of what you prayed." Well, no one knew that I had prayed about that. I didn't even *want* anyone to know I had prayed to stay home. How did this person know?

In that moment, I felt that I was standing next to an angel in disguise. I paid for our food, took our tray, and went back to the table. I said, "Denise, do you see that person over there? I think that's an angel in disguise." I told Denise about our conversation and how this person told me things no one knew but me — about how I had prayed for something to happen so I wouldn't have to leave Tulsa. I said, "Denise, I think that is an angel."

Then that person came to our table and began talking with us about the weather system that had come in. I asked, "Where are you from?" And I'll never forget the answer I received: "Heaven, of course. I'm from Heaven." I was speechless. I had "chill bumps" all over me because I realized I was standing in the presence of an angel in disguise.

This person said, "It's been wonderful to see you," then turned and walked out the front door. Denise said, "I'm going to follow that person," but when she got out the door, there was no one there.

God cares about you so much that He has assigned angels to minister to your physical and tangible needs. He has assigned angels to help you when you're physically depleted. But that's not all angels will do for you! They also provide supernatural guidance.

Supernatural Guidance

Joseph — the Earthly Father of Jesus

There are examples in both the Old and New Testaments of angels providing supernatural guidance. In Matthew 2:13, we see one such example. An angel appeared to Joseph in a dream and told him to quickly take Mary and the young Christ Child into Egypt because Herod would seek to kill the child. Most angelic supernatural guidance occurs during dreams and visions and that is demonstrated in this passage:

> **And when they were departed, behold, the angel of the Lord appeareth to Joseph in a dream, saying, Arise, and take the young child and his mother, and flee into Egypt, and be thou there until I bring thee word: for Herod will seek the young child to destroy him.**
> **— Matthew 2:13**

Notice the angel said, "…And be thou there *until I bring thee word,*" which means this angel was going to show up to give him guidance *again* in the future.

Herod was seeking Jesus to destroy Him. Later when Herod died, the same angel appeared to Joseph in a dream again — this time in Egypt informing him that Herod was dead and that he and his family could now return home to Israel. We read this in Matthew 2:19 and 20, which says, "But when Herod was dead, behold, an angel of the Lord appeareth in a dream to Joseph in Egypt, saying, Arise, and take the young child and his mother, and go into the land of Israel: for they are dead which sought the young child's life."

Philip — the Evangelist

In both Matthew 2:13 and Matthew 2:19 and 20, the supernatural angelic guidance came to Joseph in a dream. But there are examples in the New Testament of angels appearing in *physical form* to provide supernatural direction. The book of Acts records the account of an angel in disguise — who did *not* appear in a dream — and spoke to Philip the evangelist, telling him to turn south from Jerusalem toward Gaza. Acts 8:26 says, "And the angel of the Lord spake unto Philip, saying, Arise, and go toward the south unto the way that goeth down from Jerusalem unto Gaza, which is desert."

It is interesting to note that the text doesn't say that the angel told Philip *why* he was to do this. Philip could have said, "I'm not going to do it; you haven't told me why." Sometimes God doesn't give us the whole picture. And in this particular instance, all Philip was told to do was go south. And after following the guidance provided by the angel, Philip turned south and soon he met a powerful Ethiopian eunuch who served under the queen of Ethiopia. We read about this event in Acts 8:27-31 and 37-40.

> **And he [Philip] arose and went: and, behold, a man of Ethiopia, an eunuch of great authority under Candace queen of the Ethiopians, who had the charge of all her treasure, and had come to Jerusalem for to worship, was returning, and sitting in his chariot read Esaias [Isaiah] the prophet. Then the Spirit said unto Philip....**
>
> **— Acts 8:27-29**

Sometimes you must be in the right place before you receive the next instruction. First, Philip was told to go south. He did that, and once he was in the right place, he received the next step. That is very often the way God speaks to us. The Bible goes on to say in Acts 8:29-31:

> **Then the Spirit said unto Philip, Go near, and join thyself to this chariot. And Philip ran thither to him, and heard him read the prophet Esaias, and said, Understandest thou what thou readest? And he said, How can I, except some man should guide me? And he desired Philip that he would come up and sit with him.**

Philip sat with the eunuch and began to explain what he had been reading in the book of Esaias. Philip told him all about Jesus and how He had died, how Jesus had been resurrected and that He was Lord of all, and that Jesus was, in fact, the Messiah. Verses 37 through 39 continue, saying:

> **And Philip said, If thou believest with all thine heart, thou mayest. And he answered and said, I believe that Jesus Christ is the Son of God. And he commanded the chariot to stand still: and they went down both into the water, both Philip and the eunuch; and he baptized him. And when they were come up out of the water, the Spirit of the Lord *caught away* Philip, that the eunuch saw him no more....**

The words "caught away" come from the same Greek word translated "caught up" — referring to the rapture — in First Thessalonians 4:17, which means *in that split moment* Philip was caught away supernaturally. He was transported by the Holy Spirit somewhere else, and *instanta-neously*, this eunuch no longer saw him; Philip disappeared right before his eyes.

> **And when they were come up out of the water, the Spirit of the Lord caught away Philip, that the eunuch saw him no more: and he went on his way rejoicing. But Philip was found at Azotus: and passing through he preached in all the cities, till he came to Caesarea.**
>
> **— Acts 8:39,40**

At the precise moment this eunuch was reading the book of Isaiah, Philip showed up. The influential man was longing for someone to explain the Scriptures to him, and God heard the cry of this unsaved man. An angel was sent to provide supernatural guidance to Philip so he would turn south and get in position for his next word of instruction. And because Philip listened and obeyed, the eunuch was saved and was immediately baptized in water.

Cornelius — the Centurion

We find another example in Acts 10. While Cornelius the centurion was praying, an angel appeared unto him and told him to call for Peter and the other apostles to come down from Joppa to him. Because Cornelius listened to what the angel told him — and because Peter really believed that an angel had spoken to him — Peter came. He preached in the household of Cornelius and that moment changed history forever. As Peter preached, the people believed the Word of God and were saved; the Holy Spirit fell on them, they were baptized in the Holy Spirit, and the people spoke with other tongues. This was the Gentile Pentecost — the first time in Scripture a Gentile was born again. And all of it began with an angel who appeared to Cornelius the centurion and gave him supernatural guidance.

Activating Angelic Assistance

In the New Testament — particularly Matthew, Mark, Luke, John, and the book of Acts — you will find accounts of angels providing supernatural guidance. Sometimes it was by dreams and visions and sometimes angels appeared physically. Either way, according to Hebrews 1:14, angels were sent forth with the sacred task of ministering to the various needs in the lives of the heirs of salvation — the believers.

In Lesson 1, we learned that angels have been sent forth to meet physical and tangible needs and to strengthen the weary. In this lesson, we learned that angels can provide supernatural guidance. But how do we activate this help? Psalm 103:20 tells us:

Bless the Lord, ye his angels, that excel in strength, that do his commandments, hearkening unto the voice of his word.

Angels do His commandments, and when you quote the Word of God and remind the angels that they have a responsibility to provide guidance to you, they're activated. That is part of the ministry of angels that is available to you — *right now*!

STUDY QUESTIONS

Study to shew thyself approved unto God, a workman that needeth not to be ashamed, rightly dividing the word of truth.
— 2 Timothy 2:15

1. Read Matthew 2:20 and 21. The angel appeared to Joseph twice, providing instructions for Joseph and his family. What could have been the consequences of Joseph not immediately obeying the instructions he received?

2. Read Acts 8:27-40. Did the angel who appeared with directions for Philip the evangelist provide an explanation for *why* Philip was to take those next steps? What were the results of Philip's obedience?

3. Read Acts 10:1-48. How did Peter respond to the instruction he received from an angel? Did he promptly obey? Did he delay? Did he argue with the angel?

PRACTICAL APPLICATION

But be ye doers of the word, and not hearers only, deceiving your own selves.
— James 1:22

1. Have you ever delayed in following the leading of the Holy Spirit? Did it cost you anything: time, money, relationships, etc.? What did you learn from that experience? How has that experience influenced how you plan to respond to the Lord's leading in the future?

2. We learned that sometimes you must be in the right place before you receive the next instruction. And sometimes that means going back to the last thing you know the Holy Spirit instructed you to do and completing that assignment before you're able to receive the next series of steps you are to take. What was the last thing you were led by the Lord to do? Did you do it? What were the results of your obedience or disobedience? If you did not obey, take some time to repent and make the determination to carry out those instructions as soon as possible. If you did obey, what is the Holy Spirit speaking to your heart to do next?

3. In Psalm 103:20, we see how angelic assistance is activated. Have you been consistently speaking scriptures that pertain to your situation, confident that angels are activated every time you speak God's Word? Knowing this truth found in Psalm 103:20, which steps do you need to take in order to adjust your approach to applying the Word of God to your circumstances?

LESSON 3

TOPIC
Angels Provide Protection and Deliverance

SCRIPTURES

1. **Hebrews 1:14** — Are they [angels] not all ministering spirits, sent forth to minister for them who shall be heirs of salvation?
2. **Hebrews 12:22** — ...innumerable....
3. **Psalm 34:7** — The angel of the Lord encampeth round about them that fear him, and delivereth them.
4. **Psalm 91:11** — For he shall give his angels charge over thee, to keep thee in all thy ways.
5. **Acts 5:17-19** — Then the high priest rose up, and all they that were with him, (which is the sect of the Sadducees,) and were filled with indignation. And laid their hands on the apostles, and put them in the

common prison. But the angel of the Lord by night opened the prison doors, and brought them forth….

6. **Acts 12:1-3** — Now about that time Herod the king stretched forth his hands to vex certain of the church. And he killed James the brother of John with the sword. And because he saw it pleased the Jews, he proceeded further to take Peter also….

7. **Acts 12:4** — …four quaternions of soldiers….

8. **Acts 12:6,7** — And when Herod would have brought him forth, the same night Peter was sleeping between two soldiers, bound with two chains: and the keepers before the door kept the prison. And, behold, the angel of the Lord came upon him, and a light shined in the prison: and he smote Peter on the side, and raised him up, saying, Arise up quickly. And his chains fell off from his hands.

GREEK WORDS

1. "ministering" — λειτουργικός (*leitourgikos*): sacred ministry, depicting service to God and to others; one who is authorized to do sacred service, such as Old Testament priests who were to assist with the various needs of those in the temple; hence, God has assigned to angels the sacred task of serving the various needs of those who are heirs of salvation

2. "sent forth" — ἀποστέλλω (*apostello*): dispatched on assignment to represent a high-ranking power; one empowered to carry out the specific duties that are assigned to him

3. "minister" — διακονία (*diakonia*): a high-level servant; a sophisticated and highly trained servant who served the needs of others; a servant whose primary responsibility was to serve food and wait on tables; pictures a waiter or waitress who painstakingly attends to the needs, wishes, and desires of his or her client; servants who professionally pleased clients; a type of serving that was honorable, pleasurable, and done in a fashion that made the people being served feel as if they were nobility

SYNOPSIS

Supernatural deliverance is an essential aspect of the ministry God has assigned to the heavenly hosts. According to Hebrews 1:14, this is a sacred ministry that God has entrusted to the angels to carry out on behalf of every believer.

The emphasis of this lesson:

If you are an heir of salvation, angels have been sent forth to protect you, bring you out of trouble, and deliver you from destruction.

High-Level Service

In the previous two lessons, we learned that angels meet physical and tangible needs, provide strength to the weary, and give guidance to believers. Angels are entrusted with the care of the *elect* and the *heirs of salvation*. That means *YOU!* We read about this in the anchor verse, Hebrews 1:14, which says:

> **Are they** [angels] **not all ministering spirits, sent forth to minister for them who shall be heirs of salvation?**

To review, the word "ministering" was also used in the Old Testament Greek Septuagint to describe *the priests charged with assisting worshipers in the temple with various needs.* Angels have received the sacred ministry of meeting the needs of worshipers — *the elect.*

The phrase "sent forth" is translated from the Greek word *apostello,* which describes *one that is dispatched on an assignment to represent a high-ranking power.* It also depicts *one empowered to carry out a specific duty assigned to him.* This means angels have been dispatched on assignment to represent a high-ranking power — Almighty God — and they've been empowered to carry out specific duties concerning you.

The word "minister" is translated from the Greek word *diakonia,* which describes *a high-level servant* or *a sophisticated and highly trained servant who serves the needs of others.* It pictures *a waiter or waitress who painstakingly attends to the needs, wishes, and desires of his or her client, a servant whose profession it was to please clients,* or a type of serving that was *honorable, pleasurable, and done in a fashion that made the people being served feel as if they were nobility.* This means angels are highly trained, they've been sent forth to professionally serve you, and they have been commissioned to meet your needs and desires — and to treat you like nobility. Angelic ministry is not sloppy!

The primary assignments of angels are to meet the needs of God's people, strengthen the weary, give supernatural guidance, provide protection and deliverance from harm, carry out super-human feats, make special announcements, release divine judgment, and worship. In the previous two lessons, we covered three of the primary assignments of angels: to meet physical needs, to provide strength, and to give guidance.

Angels Provide Strength and Minister to Physical Needs

When Jesus concluded his 40-day fast in the wilderness, a number of angels appeared to Him to meet His physical needs. We read about this in Matthew 4:11 which says, "Then the devil leaveth him and, behold, angels came and ministered unto him."

In Luke, we see how Jesus was alone and under great pressure in the Garden of Gethsemane:

> **And there appeared an angel unto him from heaven, strengthening him.**
> **— Luke 22:45**

The word translated "strengthen" is from the Greek word *enischuo* which is a compound of the words *en*, which means *in*, and *ischuo* which means *might* or *strength*. The word *ischuo* depicts *men of great muscular abilities* like champions or heroes, but when these two words are compounded, the new word — *enischuo* — means *to impart strength, to empower, to fill a person with physical vigor*, and *to give someone renewed vitality*. It depicts a person who may have been feeling exhausted or depleted, but suddenly he receives a robust blast of energy that instantly charges him so he can continue on.

Angels Give Supernatural Guidance

In Matthew 2:13, we see an example of when an angel came to provide supernatural guidance. An angel appeared to Joseph in a dream and told him to quickly take Mary and Jesus into Egypt because Herod would seek to kill the child:

> **And when they were departed, behold, the angel of the Lord appeareth to Joseph in a dream, saying, Arise, and take the young child and his mother, and flee into Egypt, and be thou**

**there until I bring thee word: for Herod will seek the young
child to destroy him.**

— Matthew 2:13

There are examples in the New Testament of angels appearing in *physical
form* to provide supernatural direction too. Acts 8:26 says, "And the angel
of the Lord spake unto Philip, saying, Arise, and go toward the south unto
the way that goeth down from Jerusalem unto Gaza, which is desert."

After following the guidance provided by the angel, Philip turned south,
and soon he met a powerful Ethiopian eunuch who served under the
queen of Ethiopia (*see* Acts 8:27-31; 37-40).

At the precise moment this influential man was reading the book of
Isaiah, Philip showed up. This man was longing for someone to explain
the Scriptures to him, and God heard the cry of this unsaved man and
sent an angel to provide supernatural guidance to Philip so he would turn
south and get in position for his next word of instruction. And because
Philip listened and obeyed, the eunuch was saved and was immediately
baptized in water.

An Innumerable Company of Angels

Hebrews 12:22 tells us there is an "innumerable" company of angels in the
church. If there is an innumerable company, you should not be surprised
if one or two angels show up to serve you! And Hebrews 13:2 informs
us that sometimes angels appear to us in the form of humans. It exhorts,
"Be not forgetful to entertain strangers: for thereby some have entertained
angels unawares." Sometimes angels disguise themselves as people —
similar to the one in Rick's angelic encounter described in the previous
lesson.

Supernatural Angelic Deliverance

Psalm 34:7 says, "The angel of the Lord encampeth round about them
that fear him, and delivereth them." This means that if you fear the Lord,
the angel of the Lord is encamped around you. He's there all the time, and
part of his job is to deliver you. Psalm 91:11 says it this way:

**For he shall give his angels charge over thee, to keep thee in all
thy ways.**

The Apostles

We see a New Testament example of angelic deliverance in Acts 5:17-19, which says, "Then the high priest rose up, and all they that were with him, (which is the sect of the Sadducees), and were filled with indignation, and laid their hand on the apostles, and put them in the common prison. But the angel of the Lord by night opened the prison doors, and brought them forth...."

These Sadducees were angry with the apostles because a miracle had been worked. They did not believe in the supernatural, so they were infuriated that miracles had taken place. Peter and the other apostles were put into prison, and then something supernatural happened — an angel was dispatched to bring them out. The angel came to minister to those who were the *heirs of salvation* — the apostles in this instance — and gave them protection and divine deliverance and set them free.

This is what angels will do for *you* when you're in a tight place or in trouble. If you are an *heir of salvation*, angels have been sent forth to protect you, bring you out, and deliver you. So rather than saying, "I'm in such a bad place," make the decision to activate those angels by speaking the Word of God. Remind them what they're supposed to do — which is hearken to the voice of God's Word — and the moment you speak the Word of God, their assistance will be activated, and they'll go to work to bring you out of trouble!

The Apostle Peter

Another New Testament example of angelic deliverance is found in Acts 12:1-3. It says:

> **Now about that time Herod the king stretched forth his hands to vex certain of the church. And he killed James the brother of John with the sword. And because he saw it pleased the Jews, he proceeded further to take Peter also....**

According to this account, Herod had ordered the beheading of James, and he was coming for Peter next. He wanted to have Peter slaughtered, but the authorities likely remembered the last time the apostles were imprisoned, and an angel broke them out. (*See* Acts 5:19.) This time, they wanted to make sure Peter wouldn't escape, so they "delivered him to four quaternions of soldiers" (Acts 12:4).

A "quaternion" is *a group of four Roman soldiers,* and in verse 4, we see that four different groups — made up of four soldiers each — successfully took turns guarding Peter throughout the four watches of the night. That means, in total, there were 16 heavily armed Roman soldiers who were assigned to guard Peter on that particular night. But just as Psalm 34:7 says, Peter had an invisible guard that none of those soldiers were able to see — and that guard was far more powerful than the other 16 Roman soldiers combined. An angel of the Lord was encamped around Peter.

This angel was there to deliver Peter, and we see what happened next in Acts 12:6 and 7:

> **And when Herod would have brought him forth, the same night Peter was sleeping between two soldiers, bound with two chains: and the keepers before the door kept the prison. And, behold, the angel of the Lord came upon him, and a light shined in the prison: and he smote Peter on the side, and raised him up, saying, Arise up quickly. And his chains fell off from his hands.**

There Peter was, sleeping between two prison guards while two others stood watch at the prison door, when suddenly the angel of the Lord that was encamped around him appeared in the prison cell and awoke Peter from his sleep. The angel told him to rise quickly and get out of that prison, and instantly, the chains that had held Peter captive fell to the ground. Then the angel told Peter to put on his clothes and follow him — and Peter obeyed.

We see in Acts 12:6 and 7 that not only did the angel of the Lord set Peter free from the chains that held him, but it seems the angel also temporarily blinded the guards so they couldn't see Peter's escape. Peter followed the angel through two sets of doors, and when he came to the heavy iron gate, it supernaturally opened in front of him of its own accord. It also seems Peter didn't realize all of this was really happening until he found himself standing out on the street — completely free. *Amazing!* That angel delivered Peter from the horrible destiny that awaited him at the hands of Herod.

A Sacred Task

Supernatural deliverance is an essential part of the ministry that God has assigned to the heavenly hosts to give His people. The Bible says in

Hebrews 1:14, "Are they [angels] not all ministering spirits...." Again, the word "ministry" describes *sacred ministry*, and it was used in the Old Testament to describe *the ministry of priests in the temple who were to assist the various needs of worshipers.* The use of this word tells us that angels have received a sacred task — the assignment of meeting the various needs of God's people. It goes on to say they've been "sent forth." They've been specifically dispatched to minister to the heirs of salvation. And the word "minister" describes a highly trained servant who comes to professionally serve those who are around the table.

If you are saved, then you're sitting around the table of salvation, and angels have been sent forth to professionally serve you and to make you feel like royalty.

We read in Psalm 103:20 that angels "excel in strength." The fact that they are strong may be obvious to you, but simply *knowing* this information is not enough to activate angels to use that strength on your behalf. This verse goes on to say that angels "hearken to the voice of his word." They respond when they hear a prayer of faith or hear the Word of God.

An Angelic Encounter

In the program, Rick shared another example of an angelic encounter:

> Many, many years ago, I felt the leading of the Lord to go to Vorkuta — the northernmost city in the entire world above the Arctic Circle — where Joseph Stalin sent many Christians to work in the coal mines and many of them died for their faith. In fact, it seemed that several million people died in the city of Vorkuta. It is a very desolate place and I have been there many times.
>
> As far as the human eye can see, there is grave, after grave, after grave. I've seen the railroad tracks that believers built; I've been in the coal mines where they worked. It's stunning to see what happened to God's people in the city of Vorkuta.
>
> I was headed to Vorkuta to conduct some meetings and to negotiate for television time, and on our way to the airport, we stopped at a restaurant to have lunch. While we were there, I picked up a newspaper and read about how pilots had been dangerously overloading aircraft, and many recent plane crashes were due to

the fact that pilots had accepted these bribes and allowed planes to be overloaded. I read that just before I went to the airport!

We boarded the aircraft, and from where I was seated at the very front of the plane, I could see all the way to the back. And since I was seated by the door, I could also see what was happening just outside. When people started boarding the plane, I noticed that they were carrying way too much luggage to fit in the cabin. In fact, they had so overloaded the aircraft, *just like I had read in the newspaper*, that they had to bring out a whole team of people to push the cargo bay door closed!

Next, they began bringing additional boxes and pieces of luggage into the interior and lining the aisle from the front of the plane all the way to the back. Then I heard a flight attendant say to another, "I'm going to get off this plane. This plane is going to crash. This plane is overloaded. I'm getting off this plane."

I knew the Lord had told me to go to Vorkuta, so as I sat there listening to their conversation and thinking about what I'd just read in the newspaper, I said, "Lord, according to Psalm 91:11, Your angels have been sent forth to keep me in all my ways, and I'm asking for those angels to do something to protect me. I'm on assignment; I know I'm supposed to be on this plane. I'm asking You to do something to protect me."

Within minutes, the same flight attendant who had said *I'm going to get off this plane*, got on the speaker system and said, "Everybody, get off the plane as fast as you can. We just received a phone call from someone who says there's a bomb on this plane." And from where I was seated, I could see people jumping to crawl over the boxes in the aisle to get off the plane. In fact, *I* couldn't get off the plane because people were fighting and struggling to get off, and I couldn't even get out the door!

After I finally made it off the plane, everyone went back to the terminal in the airport and waited as they took everything off the plane and searched the entire aircraft. Hours later, an announcement was made that we would be re-boarding because no bomb was found. And that this time they would not be allowing the plane to be overloaded.

When I got back to my seat on the plane, I looked back and saw a completely different picture. The airplane was not overloaded, and people were peaceful; it was a completely different situation. That's when I realized an *angel* had called the airport and said there was a bomb on board. The angel took action to make sure we would be on that plane and that it was cleared of excess cargo — *completely safe*. An angel in disguise, using a human voice, protected and delivered me!

That's part of the ministry of angels to those who are the heirs of salvation (*see* Hebrews 1:14)! Yes, *you* can claim that angels will protect *you* and deliver *you*. But it's not enough to simply know that angels are present; you need to know how to *activate* their service to you. God has made this provision of angelic assistance for believers, and when you speak the Word of God, you activate the power and protection that God has made available to you.

STUDY QUESTIONS

Study to shew thyself approved unto God, a workman that needeth not to be ashamed, rightly dividing the word of truth.
— 2 Timothy 2:15

1. Who are the "heirs of salvation" mentioned in Hebrews 1:14?
2. According to Psalm 91:11 and 12, what are the angels of the Lord tasked to do for you?
3. In Acts 5:11-18, why were the Sadducees angry with the apostles?

PRACTICAL APPLICATION

But be ye doers of the word, and not hearers only, deceiving your own selves.
— James 1:22

1. Rather than be caught off guard in a dangerous situation, why not be prepared by filling your heart with the Word of God concerning angelic protection and deliverance? Take some time to write out Psalm 37:4 and Psalm 91:11 and memorize them. For out of the abundance of the heart, the mouth speaketh (*see* Matthew 12:34).

2. Write about a time you know an angel was (or may have been) activated to deliver you from trouble. Did you know at the time that an angel had been sent to deliver you?

TOPIC

Angels Make Divine Announcements and Release God's Divine Judgment

SCRIPTURES

1. **Hebrews 1:14** — Are they [angels] not all ministering spirits, sent forth to minister for them who shall be heirs of salvation?
2. **Hebrews 12:22** — …innumerable….
3. **Luke 1:34** — …How shall this be, seeing I know not a man?
4. **1 Peter 1:12** — Unto whom it was revealed, that not unto themselves, but unto us they did minister the things, which are now reported unto you by them that have preached the gospel unto you with the Holy Ghost sent down from heaven; which things the angels desire to look into.
5. **Revelation 14:6,7** — And I saw another angel fly in the midst of heaven, having the everlasting gospel to preach unto them that dwell on the earth, and to every nation, and kindred, and tongue, and people, saying with a loud voice Fear God, and give glory to him for the hour of his judgment is come: and worship him that made heaven, and earth, and the sea, and the fountains of waters.
6. **Psalm 103:20** — Bless the Lord, ye his angels, that excel in strength, that do his commandments, hearkening unto the voice of his word.

GREEK WORDS

1. "ministering" — λειτουργικός (*leitourgikos*): sacred ministry, depicting service to God and to others; one who is authorized to do sacred service, such as Old Testament priests who were to assist with the various needs of those in the temple; hence, God has assigned to angels

the sacred task of serving the various needs of those who are heirs of salvation

2. "sent forth" — ἀποστέλλω (*apostello*): dispatched on assignment to represent a high-ranking power; one empowered to carry out the specific duties that are assigned to him

3. "minister" — διακονία (*diakonia*): a high-level servant; a sophisticated and highly trained servant who served the needs of others; a servant whose primary responsibility was to serve food and wait on tables; pictures a waiter or waitress who painstakingly attends to the needs, wishes, and desires of his or her client; servants who professionally pleased clients; a type of serving that was honorable, pleasurable, and done in a fashion that made the people being served feel as if they were nobility

SYNOPSIS

Two important tasks given to angels are to make divine announcements and to initiate divine judgment. The Bible is full of examples of angels who made word-for-word announcements or released God's judgment.

The emphasis of this lesson:

There is a big difference between teaching or preaching and announcing or declaring. One is the supernatural privilege given to mankind and the other is the divine assignment given to angels.

A Quick Review

In the previous lessons, we learned that angels meet physical and tangible needs, provide strength to the weary, give guidance, and provide protection and deliverance. According to Hebrews 1:14, angels are entrusted with the task of taking care of you—the *elect* and an *heir of salvation*:

Are they [angels] not all ministering spirits, sent forth to minister for them who shall be heirs of salvation?

Once again, the word "ministering" depicts *sacred ministry*, and it was also used in the Old Testament Greek Septuagint to describe *the priests charged with assisting worshipers with various needs*. Angels have received the sacred ministry of meeting the needs of worshipers — the *elect*. And the phrase "sent forth" is translated from the Greek word *apostello*, which describes one that is dispatched on an assignment to represent a high-ranking power — in this case, Almighty God. It also depicts *one empowered to carry out a specific duty assigned to him.*

The word "minister" is translated from the Greek word *diakonia*, which describes *a high-level servant* or *a sophisticated and highly trained servant who serves the needs of others.* It pictures *a waiter or waitress who painstakingly attends to the needs, wishes, and desires of his or her client, a servant whose profession it was to please clients,* or a type of serving that was *honorable, pleasurable, and done in a fashion that made the people being served feel as if they were nobility.*

When angels come to serve, they don't do it sloppily. They are highly trained, polished, cultured, and professional. And they know how to meet the needs of those who are gathered around the table — the *heirs of salvation.* If you have called Jesus the Lord of your life, you are a born-again heir of salvation.

Hebrews 12:22 tells us there is an "innumerable" company of angels in the church. You should not be surprised if one or two show up to serve you! The primary assignments of angels are to meet the needs of God's people, strengthen the weary, give supernatural guidance, provide protection and deliverance from harm, carry out super-human feats, make special announcements, release divine judgment, and worship. In this lesson, we will see how angels make divine announcements and release God's divine judgment.

Angels Make Divine Announcements

One of the tasks of angels is to make divine announcements. Please know this does *not* mean they teach, preach, correct, or rebuke; that is the assignment given to mankind and the five-fold ministry. Humans are to *listen* to and *study* the Word of God, *pray* according to the Word of God, *digest* and *apply* the Word of God to their own lives, and then under the anointing of the Holy Spirit, they are to *preach* the Word of God. Again, teaching, preaching, correcting, and rebuking are tasks assigned solely to human beings.

Angels are not teachers, and angels are not preachers. In fact, from New Testament times to the present time, most cults have begun with some kind of angelic teaching. But according to the Bible, angels are not assigned to teach, and if you hear that an angel showed up with a teaching or a preaching subject, you need to be very leery because that is not the assignment given to angels.

Instead, angels listen and speak verbatim — *word for word* — what God has instructed them to speak. A human being has the ability to speak from what he or she has processed and elaborate on what God has shown him or her. But angels do not have that ability; they're repeaters, not preachers. Once an angel has delivered the message to someone exactly as God dictated it, the angel disappears just as quickly as it appeared.

Twice in the New Testament, we see an angel who seemed to be conversing with an individual, but this is very rare. The first was with Zacharias, who was the father of John the Baptist, and the other was with the Virgin Mary, the mother of Jesus. The angel Gabriel appeared to the young virgin and made a verbatim announcement, just as he heard it from the mouth of God, that she would give birth to Jesus. Then in Luke 1:34, we see Mary's response to this news: "How shall this be, seeing I know not a man?"

Then Gabriel answered her and clarified that this would be a miraculous birth (*see* Luke 1:35). As God's angelic messenger, Gabriel was only permitted to speak verbatim or to make a word-for-word announcement of what God had told him to speak. Once he completed his task, he disappeared because his function as an archangel was to repeat the exact message that God had given him — nothing more.

Again, as humans, we're commanded to teach and preach. And in order to do that, we must pray, study, and process what we have received. Then, under the anointing of the Holy Spirit, we are to elaborate to the best of our ability what we have seen in the Word of God. It is *our* responsibility. But angels, even with all their great supernatural abilities, cannot grasp the idea of teaching and preaching. In fact, angels are so amazed at human beings' ability to teach and preach the Word, that according to First Peter 1:12, we're told that angels hover low to watch, mesmerized by the teaching and preaching of the Bible.

> **Unto whom it was revealed, that not unto themselves, but unto us they did minister the things, which are now reported unto you by them that have preached the gospel unto you with the Holy Ghost sent down from heaven; which things the angels desire to look into.**
>
> **— 1 Peter 1:12**

When the Bible says the angels "desire to look into," it means they're hanging low, their necks outstretched; they're peering with all their might to watch and listen. They're thinking, *Wow, the ability to speak the Word of God — to elaborate and process what He has said — is mesmerizing!* They don't have that ability. Remember, angels are repeaters, not preachers.

The Bible is full of accounts of angels who came to make a verbatim word-for-word announcement. Some examples include:

- Luke 1:26 — Gabriel announced the birth of Jesus to Mary.
- Luke 2:9-14 — A multitude of angels announced the birth of Jesus to the shepherds.
- Matthew 28:5-7; Mark 16:6,7; and Luke 24:5-7 — Angels announced Jesus' resurrection.
- Acts 1:11 — Two angels appeared to the apostles at the time of Jesus' ascension and announced that Jesus would return in the same manner as they had seen Him go into Heaven.
- 1 Thessalonians 4:16,17 — The foretelling of the voice of the archangel that will announce the moment when believers will be caught up together to meet those who have been resurrected and meet the Lord in the air.

There is just one instance in the Bible that *seems* to refer to an angel's preaching. But when you dive a little deeper, you find he is not preaching at all. We can read about this occurrence in Revelation 14:6 and 7:

And I saw another angel fly in the midst of heaven, having the everlasting gospel to *preach* unto them that dwell on the earth and to every nation, and kindred, and tongue, and people, saying with a loud voice, Fear God, and give glory to him for the hour of his judgment is come: and worship him that made heaven, and earth, and the sea, and the fountains of waters.

The word "preach" in this context would be more properly translated *to proclaim* or *to announce*. This was not an angel who was preaching from his own heart. He was making a verbatim, word-by-word announcement. Remember, angels are repeaters — not preachers. The role of angels is not to teach or to rebuke; it is not to correct or to preach. But one of their jobs is to deliver divine announcements.

An Angelic Encounter

In the program, Rick shared another angelic encounter he has experienced:

> Just before I left the university, and before I was married, I was seeking the Lord about my future and what I was to do with my life. I laid down one day to take a nap on the couch. I reached up and turned off the lamp, but I couldn't fall asleep because I felt a presence in the apartment. I looked around the room and didn't see anyone, but I felt such a strong presence there.
>
> Suddenly, right in front of me, there materialized what looked like a man. I thought to myself, *Who is this?* — and the man answered me! He never opened his mouth, but he began to speak to me about my ministry and repeat what had been said to him. There was no conversation — just a word-for-word announcement about my having an end-time ministry.
>
> He repeated verbatim what he'd been told to say to me, and just as he came, he left. The moment he finished making this divine announcement to me about my ministry and future, he was gone. There was no room for conversation or elaboration.

Divine Judgment

There are many examples in the Old and New Testaments that demonstrate that angels are the ones who release God's judgment. One of the clearest examples is found in Acts 12, when people began to worship Herod as a god. Herod liked it so much that he encouraged it. We read about the results of his actions in verse 23:

> **And immediately the angel of the Lord smote him, because he gave not God the glory and he was eaten of worms, and gave up the ghost.**

This verse clearly says he was "eaten of worms," which is a very well-established fact, according to historical writings. Herod's death was brought about as the result of a judgment that was released onto him by an angel.

There are many verses in the book of Revelation that tell of angels releasing judgment upon the earth:

- Revelation 7:1 — Four angels are sent to release judgment upon the earth and sea.

- Revelation 8-11 — Seven angels sound seven trumpets that release seven judgments upon the earth.

- Revelation 14:17-20 — An angel swings a sharp sickle on the earth that releases great wrath.

- Revelation 15-16 — Seven angels pour out judgment from seven bowls onto the earth and its inhabitants.

When we read about the rapture of the church in First Thessalonians 4, we discover the voice of the archangel will sound and he will blast the trumpet. The word "trumpet" is from the Greek word *salpings*, and it describes a war cry or the blast that signifies the battle has begun. The moment the Church is released, that blast will initiate an outpouring — the release of divine judgments upon the earth.

Activating Angelic Help

So how do you access divine angelic assistance? Psalm 103:20 says, "Bless the Lord, ye his angels that excel in strength that do his commandments, hearkening unto the voice of his word."

In Rick's personal experience, he was seeking the face of God about his future by praying and quoting scriptures about the Lord speaking to him and revealing His plan. The speaking of those scriptures activated angelic ministry and he received a word-for-word announcement from the mouth of an angel.

But when it comes to judgment, you don't need to release it onto your enemies. If someone is giving you trouble, simply begin to quote the scriptures about God dealing with your enemies. The moment you begin to speak His Word, the angels will hearken to the voice of that Word, and they'll go to work. Keep your heart pure; keep your heart free and ask God to deal with your enemies according to Scripture. And when you quote the Word of God, it will activate this particular ministry of angels on your behalf.

Angels are available to do so much for you, and according to Hebrews 1:14, it is their sacred assignment to minister to the various needs of those who are heirs of salvation. Angels are highly trained, cultured, polished, and professional servants. They've come to serve those who are seated around the table — and that's *you* if Jesus is the Lord of your life. As an heir of salvation, you qualify for angelic ministry, and by speaking the Word of God, you activate their amazing service on your behalf.

STUDY QUESTIONS

Study to shew thyself approved unto God, a workman that needeth not to be ashamed, rightly dividing the word of truth.
— 2 Timothy 2:15

1. Angels have *not* been given the tasks of teaching, preaching, correcting, or rebuking humanity, but who *has* been given this ministry?
2. On two occasions in the New Testament, we see an angel who seems to be conversing with an individual. According to Luke 1, who were the two people?
3. Read Acts 12:18-23. What did Herod do that brought about the judgment of God?

PRACTICAL APPLICATION

But be ye doers of the word, and not hearers only, deceiving your own selves.
— James 1:22

1. Read First Peter 1:12. Knowing that angels are mesmerized by our ability to teach and preach the Word of God, how does this affect your perspective on the privilege given to mankind to teach and preach?
2. Do you have any enemies? Read Romans 12:19-21. Have you followed these instructions, or have you tried to issue judgment yourself to those who have wronged you? Pray and ask the Lord to help you keep your heart pure and free of all grudges and make the decision to allow Him to handle all judgment.

TOPIC

Angels Perform Superhuman Feats and Worship God

SCRIPTURES

1. **Hebrews 1:14** — Are they [angels] not all ministering spirits, sent forth to minister for them who shall be heirs of salvation?

2. **Hebrews 12:22** — …innumerable….

3. **Matthew 28:2** — …The angel of the Lord descended from heaven, and came back and rolled back the stone from the door, and sat upon it.

4. **Revelation 20:1-3** — And I saw an angel come down from heaven, having the key of the bottomless pit and a great chain in his hand. And he laid hold on the dragon, that old serpent, which is the Devil, and Satan, and bound him a thousand years, and cast him into the bottomless pit, and shut him up, and set a seal upon him, that he should deceive the nations no more, till the thousand years should be fulfilled: and after that he must be loosed a little season.

5. **Psalm 103:20** — Bless the Lord, ye his angels, that excel in strength, that do his commandments, hearkening unto the voice of his word.

6. **Job 38:7** — When the morning stars sang together, and all the sons of God shouted for joy?

7. **Deuteronomy 32:43** (*NLT*) — Rejoice with him, you heavens, and let all of God's angels worship him….

8. **Isaiah 6:1-3** — In the year that king Uzziah died I saw also the Lord sitting upon a throne, high and lifted up, and his train filled the temple. Above it stood the seraphims: each one had six wings; with twain he covered his face, and with twain he covered his feet, and with twain he did fly. And one cried unto another, and said, Holy, holy, holy, is the Lord of hosts: the whole earth is full of his glory.

9. **Hebrews 1:4-6** — Being made so much better than the angels, as he hath by inheritance obtained a more excellent name than they. For unto which of the angels said he at any time, Thou art my Son, this day have I begotten thee? And again, I will be to him a Father, and he shall be

to me a Son? And again, when he bringeth in the firstbegotten into the world, he saith, And let all the angels of God worship him.

10. **Revelation 5:11,12** — And I beheld, and I heard the voice of many angels round about the throne and the beasts and the elders: and the number of them was ten thousand times ten thousand, and thousands of thousands; saying with a loud voice, Worthy is the Lamb that was slain to receive power, and riches, and wisdom, and strength, and honour, and glory, and blessing.

11. **Revelation 7:11,12** — And all the angels stood round about the throne, and about the elders and the four beasts, and fell before the throne on their faces, and worshipped God, saying, Amen: Blessing, and glory, and wisdom, and thanksgiving, and honour, and power, and might, be unto our God for ever and ever. Amen.

12. **Luke 2:13,14** — And suddenly there was with the angel a multitude of the heavenly host praising God, and saying, Glory to God in the highest, and on earth peace, good will toward men.

GREEK WORDS

1. "ministering" — λειτουργικός (*leitourgikos*): sacred ministry, depicting service to God and to others; one who is authorized to do sacred service, such as Old Testament priests who were to assist with the various needs of those in the temple; hence, God has assigned to angels the sacred task of serving the various needs of those who are heirs of salvation

2. "sent forth" — ἀποστέλλω (*apostello*): dispatched on assignment to represent a high-ranking power; one empowered to carry out the specific duties that are assigned to him

3. "minister" — διακονία (*diakonia*): a high-level servant; a sophisticated and highly trained servant who served the needs of others; a servant whose primary responsibility was to serve food and wait on tables; pictures a waiter or waitress who painstakingly attends to the needs, wishes, and desires of his or her client; servants who professionally pleased clients; a type of serving that was honorable, pleasurable, and done in a fashion that made the people being served feel as if they were nobility

4. "stone" — λίθος (*lithos*): a stone; however, stones placed in front of such tombs were immense in their dimensions — impossible for a human being to move without the assistance of several people

5. "sat" — **κάθημαι** (*kathemai*): to sit down

6. "worship" — **προσκυνέω** (*proskuneo*): to kiss the ground when prostrating before a superior; to fall down and prostrate oneself; to adore on one's knees; or to worship with all necessary physical gestures of worship

7. "saying" — **λέγοντες** (*legontes*): saying, saying, and saying; continuously and repeatedly saying

8. "loud voice" — **φωνῇ μεγάλῃ** (*phone megale*): the word **φωνῇ** (*phone*) means a noise, a sound, a voice, or a loud whirling; depicts the sound of wind, wings, or water; the word **μεγάλῃ** (*megale*) means great or large; as a phrase, it pictures an overwhelmingly loud sound

9. "fell before" — **πίπτω** (*pipto*): to fall or to collapse; often depicts one who falls so hard it appears he fell like a corpse; a downfall from a high position

10. "worshipped" — **προσκυνέω** (*proskuneo*): to kiss the ground when prostrating before a superior; to fall down and prostrate oneself; to adore on one's knees; or to worship with all necessary physical gestures of worship

11. "praising" — **αἰνέω** (*aineo*): to verbally laud or to verbally express praise

12. "saying" — **λεγόντων** (*legonton*): saying, saying, and saying; continuously and repeatedly saying

SYNOPSIS

The primary assignments of angels are to meet the needs of God's people, strengthen the weary, give supernatural guidance, provide protection and deliverance from harm, carry out superhuman feats, make special announcements, release divine judgment, and worship God.

The emphasis of this lesson:

There are many verses in Scripture that mention angels worshiping God. And since the word "praise" is often used, it's easy to see how some might think that means angels *sing* praises. But what does the Bible really say? In this final lesson, we will dive into the Scriptures to reveal the ways angels express worship to God.

The Divine Tasks of Angels

In the previous lessons, we learned that angels meet physical and tangible needs, provide strength to the weary, give guidance, provide protection and deliverance, make divine announcements, and release God's divine judgment. And according to Hebrews 1:14, angels are entrusted with the task of taking care of you — the *elect* and an *heir of salvation.*

Are they [angels] **not all ministering spirits, sent forth to minister for them who shall be heirs of salvation?**

As a final review, the word "ministering" refers to *sacred ministry.* It was also used in the Old Testament Greek Septuagint to describe *the priests charged with assisting worshipers in the temple with various needs.* Angels have received the sacred ministry of meeting the needs of worshipers — the *elect.* And the phrase "sent forth" is translated from the Greek word *apostello,* which describes *one that is dispatched on an assignment to represent a high-ranking power* — in this case, Almighty God. It also depicts *one empowered to carry out a specific duty assigned to him.*

The word "minister" in this verse is translated from the Greek word *diakonia,* which describes *a high-level servant* or *a sophisticated and highly trained servant who serves the needs of others.* It pictures *a waiter or waitress who painstakingly attends to the needs, wishes, and desires of his or her client, a servant whose profession it was to please clients,* or a type of serving that was *honorable, pleasurable, and done in a fashion that made the people being served feel as if they were nobility.*

These "ministers" were servants who served the tables of very wealthy people in very elegant homes, and because they were serving such prestigious people, they had to be polished, cultured, and professional in the way they served. If you are a child of God, then you have a seat at the table of salvation, and angels are available to serve *you.*

Angels also make divine announcements, but they do not teach, preach, correct, or rebuke. In fact, from New Testament times to the present, we see that most cults have begun with some kind of angelic teaching. Instead, angels listen and speak verbatim — word for word — what God has instructed them to speak. And once an angel has delivered a message to someone exactly as God dictated it, the angel disappears just as quickly as it appeared.

Hebrews 12:22 tells us there is an "innumerable" company of angels. And if there is an innumerable company, you should not be surprised if one or two show up to serve you!

Once again, the primary assignments of angels are to meet the needs of God's people, to strengthen the weary, to give supernatural guidance, to provide protection and deliverance from harm, to carry out super-human feats, to make special announcements, to release divine judgment, and to worship. In this final lesson, we will see how angels perform superhuman feats and worship God.

Angels Perform Superhuman Feats

One of the clearest examples of an angel performing a superhuman feat is found in Matthew 28:2, which says:

> **And, behold, there was a great earthquake: for the angel of the Lord descended from heaven, and came and rolled back the stone from the door, and sat upon it.**

The word "stone" is a translation of the Greek word *lithos*, which is the word for *a stone,* but in early New Testament times, the stones that were placed in front of the tombs were so enormous that they had to be rolled in grooves and required many hands to move them. They were *massive* stones. But the angel in Matthew 28:2 rolled back the stone from the door by himself and then sat on top of it. That is *amazing!*

The word "sat" is from the Greek word which means *to sit down* and describes *one sitting in a chair.* There are scholars who suggest that the angel's ability to *sit down* on top of the stone — as if sitting in a chair — indicates the size of the angel. The angel had to have been gigantic for him to be able to simply back up and sit down on top of this stone. Not only did this angel have superhuman strength to move that stone on his own, but he sat on top of it as if he were sitting in a chair.

We find another example of an angel's superhuman strength in Revelation 20:1-3, which says:

> **And I saw an angel come down from heaven, having the key of the bottomless pit and a great chain in his hand. And he laid hold on the dragon, that old serpent, which is the Devil, and Satan, and bound him a thousand years, and cast him into the**

bottomless pit, and shut him up, and set a seal upon him, that he should deceive the nations no more....

The angel mentioned in this passage was likely the archangel Michael, who we find is constantly resisting evil principalities and powers and dealing with the devil. But here we see the example of an unnamed angel seizing Satan. This angel would have to be extremely strong to be able to seize and overpower Satan. Clearly, Satan is not the most powerful being!

This angel binds Satan with a great chain, shuts him up in the bottomless pit, and seals him with the seal so he cannot escape. No human being could ever carry out a feat of such physical strength! Revelation 20:1-3 clearly describes a day that is *really coming* when an angel (possibly the archangel Michael) will *singlehandedly* accomplish this feat. This is scriptural proof of the great power that is possessed by heavenly angels.

Activating Angelic Help and Strength

In each lesson, we revisited the question of *how* to activate this angelic help because it is important that believers understand this principle. We find the answer to this question in Psalm 103:20, which says, "Bless the Lord, ye his angels, that excel in strength, that do his commandments, *hearkening unto the voice of his word.*"

According to Psalm 103:20, if you don't speak the Word of God, the angels will stand unmoving. They will not move until they hear the commandment of the Word of God. So if you're in a position where you need help, just declare Psalm 91:11 and 12:

For he shall give his angels charge over thee, to keep thee in all thy ways. They shall bear thee up in their hands, lest thou dash thy foot against a stone.

When you quote this verse, angels will *immediately* be activated to demonstrate superhuman power to protect you!

Angels Worship God

Among the other angelic tasks covered in this series, the assignment to worship has also been given to angels. It is interesting to note that there is not a single verse in the entire Bible that explicitly mentions angels *singing*. However, this does not mean angels *don't* sing. Rick mentioned on the program that once while Denise was leading praise and worship in Moscow, they suddenly heard voices that were transcendent beyond anything Rick, Denise, and the rest of the congregation could have produced with their own voices. They knew these were angels that had joined them in worship. But in the Bible, there is not one example of angels who sing — yet we do see that they do *worship*.

You may be wondering, "What about Job 38:7?" Well, let's take a look! The *King James Version* says it this way:

When the morning stars sang together, and all the sons of God shouted for joy.

The word "sang" in Hebrew means *to cry out, to give a ringing noise, to scream loudly*, or *to shout*. This word does not have anything to do with singing but rather with making a verbal declaration — they shouted for joy. The word "shouted" is a translation of a Hebrew word that means *to raise a shout as a form of applause, to give a battle cry, to shout in triumph*, or *to make a joyful shout*. Again, there is no mention of singing. The *King James* translators wrongly translated that Hebrew word to "sang" when they should have used "shouted" or "said."

Deuteronomy 32:43 (*NLT*) says, "Rejoice with him, you heavens, and let all of God's angels worship him." The word "rejoice" in this verse is the same word translated as "sang" in Job 38:7. So Deuteronomy 32:43 could have also been translated, "*Cry out* and *shout* with him, you heavens...."

And Isaiah 6:1-3 says, "In the year that king Uzziah died I saw also the Lord sitting upon a throne, high and lifted up, and his train filled the temple. Above it stood the seraphims: each one had six wings; with twain he covered his face, and with twain he covered his feet, and with twain he did fly. And one cried unto another, and said...." Notice singing is not mentioned; one *cried* and another *said*, "Holy, holy, holy is the Lord of hosts: the whole earth is full of his glory." The word "cry" in Hebrew means *to cry out, to verbally proclaim*, or *to proclaim loudly*. It also means *to verbally declare, to verbally say, to verbally utter*, and *to verbally speak*. This means the angels mentioned in Isaiah 6 were *saying* and *declaring*.

Another example is found in Hebrews 1:4-6, where it says:

Being made so much better than the angels, as he hath by inheritance obtained a more excellent name than they. For unto which of the angels said he at any time, Thou art my Son, this

day have I begotten thee? And again, I will be to him a Father, and he shall be to me a Son? And again, when he bringeth in the first begotten into the world, he saith, and let all the angels of God worship him.

The word "worship" is the Greek word *proskuneo*, which means *to kiss the ground when falling flat on the ground before a superior*. It means *to fall down, to adore on one's knees*, or *to worship with all the necessary gestures of worship*. Everything in this word has to do with physical gestures — *not* singing.

And in Revelation 5:11 and12, it says, "And I beheld, and I heard the voice of many angels round about the throne and the beasts and the elders: and the number of them was ten thousand times ten thousand, and thousands of thousands; *saying* with a loud voice, Worthy is the Lamb that was slain to receive power, and riches, and wisdom, and strength, and honour, and glory, and blessing." Again, there is no mention of angels singing in this verse.

The word "saying" here is translated from the Greek word *legontes*, which means *saying and saying and saying* or *continuously and repeatedly saying*. The angels were not singing. They were making a verbal declaration with a loud voice. The words "loud voice" in the original Greek mean *an overwhelming sound*.

Additionally, we see that Revelation 7:11 and 12 says, "And all the angels stood round about the throne, and about the elders and the four beasts, and fell before the throne on their faces, and worshipped God, *saying*, Amen: Blessing, and glory, and wisdom, and thanksgiving, and honour, and power, and might, be unto our God forever and ever. Amen."

Notice in this passage it says the angels "fell before," which is a translation from the Greek word *pipto*. This word means *to fall* or *to collapse*. It depicts *one who falls so hard that it appears he's fallen like a corpse* or *a downward fall from a high position*. These powerful angels literally collapsed in the presence of God. The verse goes on to say they "worshipped," which again, is the Greek word *proskuneo* and describes *worshiping with physical gestures*. And the word "saying" is the Greek word for *a continuous and repeated saying*.

These verses make no mention of angels singing but only making verbal declarations — that is the way they worship.

Now someone may say, "Wait! What about the angels that appeared to the shepherds at Jesus' birth?" Let's take a look at Luke 2:13 and 14:

And suddenly there was with the angel a multitude of the heavenly host praising God, and saying glory to God in the highest, and on earth peace, good will toward men.

It's understandable how one would assume the angels were singing because of our own interpretation of the word "praising." However, the word "praising" is a translation from the Greek word *aineo*, which means *to verbally laud, to verbally declare*, or *to verbally express praise*. The word "saying" is the same word in previously mentioned verses, which means *saying and saying and saying* or *continuous and repeated saying*. This is not to say angels *never* sing, but the Bible does not explicitly say that they do. However, the Bible *does* say that angels *verbally declare*. This points to the power of confession — speaking and declaring what you believe. The angels *say* and *say* and *say*. They worship and they engage their mouths to verbally declare the greatness of God. This is the way angels worship, and it is a divine assignment given to them by Almighty God!

STUDY QUESTIONS

Study to shew thyself approved unto God, a workman that needeth not to be ashamed, rightly dividing the word of truth.
— 2 Timothy 2:15

1. According to Psalm 103:20, how is the assistance of angels activated?
2. We have seen that there is no mention of angels singing anywhere in the Bible. Instead, in what way does the Bible indicate that angels worship God?

PRACTICAL APPLICATION

But be ye doers of the word, and not hearers only, deceiving your own selves.
— James 1:22

1. In Revelation 20:1-3, we see Satan's ultimate fate is to be overpowered and defeated by an unnamed archangel. How does knowing that the enemy's strength is no match for an archangel of Almighty God affect your perspective of the authority Christ has given to you as a believer?

2. Many times in Scripture, we see that angels speak and declare worship unto God. They speak and declare what they know to be true about Him. What about your own life — are the words you have been saying worthy of being considered worship unto God?

Notes

Notes

Notes

CLAIM YOUR FREE RESOURCE!

As a way of introducing you further to the teaching ministry of Rick Renner, we would like to send you FREE of charge his teaching, "How To Receive a Miraculous Touch From God" on CD or as an MP3 download.

In His earthly ministry, Jesus commonly healed *all* who were sick of *all* their diseases. In this profound message, learn about the manifold dimensions of Christ's wisdom, goodness, power, and love toward all humanity who came to Him in faith with their needs.

☑ **YES, I want to receive Rick Renner's monthly teaching letter!**

Simply scan the QR code to claim this resource or go to: **renner.org/claim-your-free-offer**

Connect

WITH US!